Original title:

The Twilight Path

Copyright © 2024 Creative Arts Management OÜ

Author: Tobias Winslow
ISBN HARDBACK: 978-9916-90-818-1
ISBN PAPERBACK: 978-9916-90-819-8

Moonlit Serenity

A silver glow on tranquil seas,
Whispers dance upon the breeze.
Night unfolds its velvet cloak,
In dreams, the world awakes and spoke.

Reflections shimmer, soft and bright,
Guiding hearts through quiet night.
Each wave, a tale of love and loss,
In moonlit calm, we count the cost.

The Edge of Dusk's Embrace

As daylight fades in crimson hues,
The sky dons its twilight blues.
Whispers of the coming night,
Wrap the world in gentle light.

Shadows stretch and mingle near,
Softly rising, never fear.
On the horizon, stars ignite,
A promise held in tender sight.

Beneath the Veil of Stars

In a canvas painted deep and wide,
Dreams and wishes there abide.
Each twinkle, a secret shared,
In the night, our hearts bared.

Beneath the veil of night so vast,
We find our treasures from the past.
Galaxies whisper, softly call,
Unraveling mysteries for all.

Where Shadows Greet the Stars

In the quiet where silence dwells,
Drawn in shadows, magic swells.
Stars appear, a guiding light,
Painting pathways through the night.

Where dreams align with the unknown,
In this realm, we are not alone.
Every heartbeat, every sigh,
Echoes softly, as night draws nigh.

Shadows Beneath the Dusk

The sun dips low beneath the trees,
Casting shadows, whispering pleas.
Colors blend in soft goodbye,
As night prepares to softly pry.

Footsteps linger on the ground,
In the hush, no other sound.
Echoes fade in twilight's grace,
Lost in time, we find our place.

Echoes of the Gloaming

In the gloaming, shadows creep,
Secrets hidden, silence deep.
Stars awaken, one by one,
Chasing dreams 'til night is done.

Whispers float on evening air,
Carried soft, a lover's prayer.
Moments stretch, then fade away,
Underneath the moon's soft sway.

Journey Through Fading Light

Beneath the sky, the colors melt,
Stories of the day are felt.
Each step leads where shadows play,
In twilight's arms, we drift away.

With gentle hands, the night draws near,
Embracing all we hold so dear.
Memories blend as darkness calls,
In fading light, the spirit thralls.

Whispers of the Evening Veil

The world slows down, a gentle sigh,
As daylight fades, we learn to fly.
Through the veil of soft twilight,
Hope ignites, a tender light.

In the stillness, hearts unite,
Wrapped in warmth, away from fright.
Together we greet the night,
With whispered dreams, our spirits bright.

A Symmetry in Shadows

In twilight's hush, shadows agree,
A dance of silhouettes set free.
With whispers soft, the night takes form,
A quiet peace, the heart grows warm.

Beneath the arch of starlit skies,
Echoes of dreams softly arise.
The moon breaks through with silver grace,
In shadows' arms, we find our place.

Emotions at Day's End

As daylight wanes, feelings collide,
A canvas brushed by waves of tide.
Each color blends with hues of time,
Whispers of dusk, a gentle rhyme.

With every sigh, the sun dips low,
Emotions stir in evening's glow.
Beneath the blush of night's embrace,
We find ourselves in quiet space.

The Soft Whisper of Darkened Woods

In darkened woods, secrets entwine,
A rustle speaks in sacred line.
Branches sway with a gentle sigh,
As creatures pause to wonder why.

Moonbeams dance on fern and stone,
Nature's voice, a whispered tone.
In stillness deep, we hear the call,
A magic thrums beneath it all.

Journey Beyond the Fading Horizon

As day gives way to night's embrace,
We wander forth, in endless space.
Each step a tale, a breath, a dream,
Beyond the line where worlds may seem.

The horizon fades, yet hope remains,
In twilight's glow, our spirit gains.
With every heartbeat, journeys start,
A voyage endless, we depart.

Echoes of Evening Light

The sun dips low, a golden hue,
Whispers of dusk, the night anew.
Shadows stretch across the fields,
A tender warmth, the world it shields.

Crickets chirp, a soft refrain,
As twilight dances on the pane.
Stars emerge, a silver song,
In evening's arms, we all belong.

Journey through the Gloaming

Footsteps whisper on the ground,
In the gloaming, magic's found.
Leaves rustle with a secret breeze,
Time suspends, the heart's at ease.

Fading light, the path unclear,
Yet there's courage, free of fear.
The horizon blurs, night takes its claim,
But still we walk, through mist, through flame.

Veils of Dusk

Softly draped in violet skies,
Where the daylight gently dies.
Each breath taken, a quiet pause,
In the stillness, a world that draws.

Veils of dusk, so sweet and true,
Brush of dreams, a gentle hue.
The stars awaken, shy and bright,
As whispers weave through the night.

Where Dreams Meet Darkness

In the folds of twilight's seam,
Lies a place where shadows dream.
Silent echoes, soft and deep,
In this realm, the worlds do leap.

Faintest stars begin to glow,
As mysteries of night unfold.
A dance of thoughts, both bright and stark,
Where dreams and darkness leave their mark.

Radiance Wanes

The sun dips low, a fading glow,
Colors blend in a gentle flow.
Whispers of night begin to rise,
As shadows dance in dusky skies.

Stars blink softly, one by one,
Marking the end of day's bright run.
Moonlight bathes the world in dreams,
As the last of daylight gently gleams.

The Lullaby of Half-Light

In the twilight where secrets bloom,
Softly wrapped in a velvet gloom.
Nature sings a soothing tune,
Beneath the watchful eye of the moon.

Crickets chirp in mellow sway,
As shadows linger, drift away.
A lullaby woven with stars,
Erasing all of the day's old scars.

Chasing Shadows Near the Horizon

Footsteps echo on sandy trails,
Chasing dreams where daylight fails.
The horizon beckons with a sigh,
Where shadows linger and whispers fly.

Fleeting moments, a soft embrace,
Solitudes wrapped in a warm place.
With each breath, the world expands,
As time slips through our eager hands.

Underneath the Pearl-Studded Sky

Night unfurls its velvet cloth,
Adorned with pearls, a starry troth.
Silent wishes drift with ease,
Carried softly on the breeze.

In the calm, dreams start to weave,
Stories hidden, hearts believe.
Underneath this cosmic show,
Hope ignites in a gentle glow.

Where the Light Bows Down

In the hush of dawn's embrace,
The shadows gently sway and bow.
Whispers of the morning grace,
As the soft light breaks the vow.

Petals dance with glistening dew,
Nature hums a healing tune.
Silence wraps the world anew,
Underneath the watching moon.

Colors blend in golden streams,
Dreams awaken, softly found.
In this magic, hope redeems,
Where the light bows down to ground.

Tides of a Darkening Sky

Waves of gray roll overhead,
As whispers of a storm arise.
The world prepares for what is fed,
By winds that weave with heavy sighs.

A sea of thoughts, both wild and free,
Crashes on the shores of night.
In depths of doubt, we seek to be,
Guided by the flickering light.

Clouds will part to share their tears,
And the stars will find their way.
Through the tempest, cast away fears,
In the arms of dawn's soft sway.

Consecrated Moments in Quietude

In stillness where the heart beats slow,
Time weaves whispers, soft and clear.
Each breath a sacred, gentle flow,
Moments held, precious and dear.

The world outside fades far away,
As echoes of the soul unwind.
Within this space, we softly play,
Finding peace in what we find.

Candles flicker with a glow,
Illuminating paths of grace.
Here in silence, we bestow,
Love that time cannot erase.

An Ode to Midsummer Nights

Underneath the velvet skies,
Laughter twirls like fireflies bright.
Dreams unfold with softest sighs,
In the warmth of midsummer light.

Stars embrace the velvet haze,
Moonlight kisses fields of green.
Voices sing in joyful praise,
A tapestry across the scene.

As twilight dances, shadows play,
Each moment lingers like a song.
In this blissful, fleeting sway,
We find a place where we belong.

Cadence of an Eclipsed Sun

In shadows cast by fleeting light,
The sun retreats, a quiet flight.
Whispers of day fade into night,
While stars awaken, taking flight.

The world hushes, a cosmic sigh,
As darkness drapes across the sky.
Time stands still, the moments lie,
In solitude, we wonder why.

Portals to the Coming Night

Through open doors, the dusk descends,
A gentle veil as daylight ends.
Each shadow stretches, softly bends,
Where silence speaks and stillness mends.

The horizon glows in amber flames,
While night reveals her secret names.
With every star, the cosmos claims,
A tapestry of whispered dreams.

The Embrace of Faint Luminescence

In twilight's grip, a soft embrace,
Faint glimmers dance in outer space.
A fragile glow, a timeless chase,
Where hopes emerge, our fears replace.

Across the sky, the echoes swell,
Of every wish, a secret spell.
In cosmic lullabies, we dwell,
As night unfolds her mystic well.

Fables of the Dusk

In stories told where shadows creep,
The dusk unveils its secrets deep.
Each whispered tale, a promise keep,
As twilight lingers, we softly weep.

From fading light, the legends born,
Of battles fought on fields of corn.
With every star, a heart is worn,
In timeless tales, our dreams are sworn.

The Lure of Evening Strolls

In the whispers of the trees,
Where shadows dance and tease,
Footsteps light on cobblestone,
A quiet path that feels like home.

Moonlight drapes the gentle street,
Softly guiding weary feet,
Chirping crickets serenade,
While fading colors softly fade.

Each corner holds a tale untold,
Promises of warmth and gold,
The evening air, a sweet embrace,
Inviting smiles on every face.

With every step, worries cease,
Finding solace, finding peace,
A moment cradled in the night,
The world transformed in gentle light.

Enigmas of the Dusk-kissed World

Secrets linger in the air,
Mysteries hidden everywhere,
As day gives way to twilight's glow,
Silent shadows start to grow.

Birds take flight to distant lands,
While stars unveil their ancient plans,
The horizon blurs, colors blend,
In this hour, all realms can mend.

A fleeting breeze, a haunting sigh,
Whispers of dreams that wave goodbye,
In the dusk, we ponder fate,
As time sits still, we contemplate.

What stories does the night unfold?
In its embrace, a touch of gold,
The dusk-kissed world forever spins,
Where every ending softly begins.

Veils of the Coming Night

Veils of darkness start to creep,
As weary souls begin to sleep,
The sun dips low, a final bow,
Calling forth the night's sweet vow.

Stars emerge, a sparkling font,
In the sky, their gentle haunt,
Each twinkle holds a wish or two,
A canvas painted deep and blue.

Gentle whispers through the trees,
Lulls the heart, sets minds at ease,
For in the night, we find our way,
Guided by the moon's soft sway.

Veils of night, a shroud so thin,
Invite us to the dreams within,
In shadows, secrets come to light,
In silence, we embrace the night.

A Journey in the Dwindling Light

With every step, the day recedes,
Fading softly like the reeds,
A journey in the golden hue,
Where shadows merge with thoughts anew.

The path unwinds, the stars align,
Flickers of hope in every sign,
As daylight wanes, the magic grows,
In the twilight's grasp, anything goes.

Each heartbeat echoes through the night,
In this tapestry of fading light,
A chance to pause, to breathe, to dream,
In a world that flows like a gentle stream.

As darkness falls, we wander free,
In the soft embrace of mystery,
For every ending holds a spark,
In the light that lingers in the dark.

Secrets of the Luminous Veil

In whispers soft, the shadows weave,
The tales of light that glow and leave.
Hidden truths like stars that twinkle,
In the silence where dreams can crinkle.

Veils of shimmer, soft and bright,
Guard the secrets of the night.
Echoes of laughter on the breeze,
Crafting magic through the trees.

Every flicker holds a spark,
In twilight's grasp, where whispers hark.
Dancing softly in the dark,
Untold stories leave their mark.

Beneath the glow of twilight's ray,
Secrets linger, drift away.
In the veil so luminous,
Hope blooms softly, still and thus.

Wandering through the Dimming Glow

On paths of amber, shadows play,
Wandering hearts find their way.
Through gardens where the day departs,
In the stillness, life imparts.

Fading light spills like sweet wine,
Dancing hues in a grand design.
Every step on the whispering earth,
Speaks of dreams and quiet worth.

The evening sky, a canvas spun,
Where colors meld 'til day is done.
Wandering souls, a fleeting trace,
In the glow, we find our place.

As night unfurls its velvet guise,
We wander on beneath the skies.
In each breath, a softened thrill,
With every moment, time stands still.

Hues of Dusk's Canvas

The sunset spills its fiery lore,
Painting skies with hues that soar.
Crimson, gold, and deep indigo,
In dusk's embrace, the world starts to glow.

Brushstrokes blend on twilight's frame,
Each color whispers a different name.
A symphony of light descends,
In every shade, the silence bends.

Nature's palette, rich and wide,
Holds the secrets that it hides.
Beneath the canvas, shadows play,
As dusk transforms the end of day.

In this moment, peace takes flight,
As colors fade into the night.
Each hue a memory captured fast,
In the heart, the light will last.

Beneath the Blushing Sky

Where day meets night in softest sigh,
We gather dreams beneath the sky.
Blushing clouds in shades so rare,
Whisper secrets hung in air.

Golden rays kiss twilight's bloom,
In this moment, hearts find room.
As stars begin their gentle rise,
We trace the tales in twilight's eyes.

Every breath a story shared,
In the dusk, our souls declared.
Beneath the blush, we stand as one,
In the dance of night, the day is done.

Forever marked in time's embrace,
We linger here in this sacred space.
In the glow of twilight's spark,
We find our light within the dark.

Celestial Pathways

Beneath the stars, we wander far,
Tracing dreams near Jupiter's scar.
Galaxies whisper in the night,
Guiding souls with silver light.

Comets blaze with tales untold,
Secrets in their tails unfold.
Nebulas dance in hues so bright,
A cosmic waltz under the night.

The moonbeams weave their gentle lace,
Inviting us to slow our pace.
As cosmic tides embrace the shore,
We seek the paths to wander more.

In endless skies where wonders gleam,
We find our truth within the dream.
Celestial pathways call us home,
In starlit realms, forever roam.

Surrender to the Darkening Hours

As twilight wraps the world in gray,
The sun dips low, it fades away.
Soft shadows creep across the land,
Whispers shared by night's own hand.

The stars emerge, a twinkling choir,
Each spark a hope, each pulse a fire.
In silence deep, we breathe the night,
Surrendering to lingering light.

Moonlight drapes like silver silk,
Embracing hearts, the night grows still.
In shadows cast, we find our way,
To rest our dreams till break of day.

With every breath, we find our peace,
As darkening hours bring release.
In the calm, we let go and trust,
The dawn will rise, for hope is just.

Reflections of a Fading Light

The sun retreats with weary grace,
While colors blend in soft embrace.
A shimmer fades from sky to sea,
In twilight's grasp, like memory.

Like echoes of a distant song,
The light departs, but won't be long.
In shadows cast, the past ignites,
We hold the glow of fleeting nights.

Beneath the stars, we chase the fire,
A glimmer born of pure desire.
Reflections flicker, then they cease,
Leaving echoes of sweet release.

Yet in the dark, our hopes endure,
For every ending, there's a cure.
In fading light, we find our way,
To brighter dreams that greet the day.

The Forgotten Hour

In whispers lost to time's embrace,
A clock that ticks, yet leaves no trace.
Memories fade like morning dew,
All smiles now, a distant hue.

An hour caught in twilight's veil,
Where shadows blend and spirits sail.
Silence reigns, the world stands still,
As echoes of the past fulfill.

Time forgets, but we recall,
The laughter, love, the rise, the fall.
In dreams, we roam the paths once known,
In that hour, we're never alone.

So hold the moment, lush and dear,
Embrace the whispers that you hear.
For in the folds of fate's soft hour,
Lives every soul, every flower.

Steps into the Softening Dark

As daylight wanes, the shadows grow,
A gentle hush, a softening glow.
We tread on paths where secrets lie,
Beneath the vast and starry sky.

With every step, the world unwinds,
In quiet spaces, peace we find.
The night unfolds its velvet wing,
While whispers of the evening sing.

With each breath, the dark of night,
Embraces dreams, ignites our flight.
In fleeting moments, we explore,
The heart of dusk, the night's allure.

So take my hand, let's drift away,
Into the night where shadows play.
For when we walk, the dark grows bright,
In soft embraces, peace ignites.

Soft Echoes of Fading Light

When daylight dims and colors blend,
The sun retreats, the shadows mend.
A canvas spread of gold and gray,
Where whispers of the dusk hold sway.

The echoes dance in silent air,
As night creeps in, beyond compare.
Upon the hills, the fading light,
Paints dreams anew in starry flight.

With each soft breath, the world unwinds,
While crickets sing their sweet designs.
The twilight hums, a tender song,
In fading light, we all belong.

So let the day in peace descend,
For every dusk has its sweet end.
And in the echoes of the night,
We find our hearts, our guiding light.

A Dance of Lingering Shadows

In shadows long, the night begins,
A dance of dreams, where silence spins.
Figures move with grace and poise,
In the quiet, the heart rejoices.

Beneath the moon's soft, silver gaze,
Memories swirl in a gentle haze.
With every step, the world ignites,
A ballet of soft, silent lights.

The whispers of the past entwine,
In shadows cast, our hopes align.
We twirl and spin in fleeting time,
In a rhythm pure, a silent rhyme.

So come, dear friend, let's dance anew,
In the lingering dark, where dreams pass through.
For every shadow holds a spark,
In the tender embrace of the night's arc.

Where Silence Meets the Stars

In the velvet cloak of night,
Stars whisper secrets untold.
The moon hangs like a lantern,
Casting dreams of silver and gold.

Beneath the vast celestial dome,
Hearts quietly drift away.
With every twinkle, hope is born,
In the stillness, shadows sway.

Time suspends its steady course,
As darkness wraps the earth in grace.
Each breath is deep with wonder,
As silence finds its rightful place.

Moments linger in the hush,
As thoughts collide with starry seas.
Where silence meets the stars above,
A symphony of gentle peace.

Hallowed Ground of the Evening

When dusk descends on hallowed ground,
The sky ignites in warm embrace.
Colors blend in tender light,
As shadows dance with softened grace.

Whispers of the day now fade,
As twilight sighs with gentle sighs.
Each leaf can tell a story deep,
As night prepares her velvet guise.

Time stands still, a fleeting dream,
With every star, a wish is sewn.
In this sacred, tranquil space,
We find a solace of our own.

Embrace the peace the night bestows,
In the hush of coming night.
With every breath, we journey forth,
Into the depths of starlit light.

Twilight's Mysterious Edge

At twilight's edge, the world holds breath,
A veil of magic cloaks the air.
The horizon blushes, rich and deep,
While shadows weave with tender care.

Mysteries linger, just out of reach,
Where day and night begin to blur.
Questions hang like ancient stars,
In the silence, whispers stir.

Wandering souls with wandering hearts,
Chase the fleeting moments near.
In twilight's glow, we seek the truth,
In the fading light, we find our fear.

Holding dreams as twilight fades,
We learn to dance on edges sharp.
In this sacred hour, we arise,
With every heartbeat, every spark.

The Breach of Night

In the breach of night, where shadows play,
Darkness beckons, soft and wide.
A tapestry of dreams unfolds,
As starlit wishes gently glide.

Waves of calm roll through the air,
Wrapped in night's encompassing sighs.
With every heartbeat, magic swirls,
While the moonlight gently tries.

The world slumbers, wrapped in peace,
While secrets drift on whispered song.
Each moment breathes a quiet truth,
In shadows where we all belong.

Lost in the beauty of the night,
We find our souls entwined with fate.
In the breach of night, we stand as one,
As darkness weaves, we contemplate.

Cascading into the Night

Whispers dance on evening's breath,
As shadows stretch and fade to rest.
Stars awaken, tiny sparks,
Mapping dreams in the dark.

Silhouettes of trees stand tall,
Cascading leaves, a gentle call.
Moonlight spills on silent ground,
In its glow, peace is found.

Softly echoes the nightingale,
Singing tales of lovers' wail.
In the quiet, hearts take flight,
Cascading into blissful night.

Every moment, pure delight,
Wrapped in the arms of sheer twilight.
Embracing what the darkness brings,
Through the night, our spirit sings.

Sketches of a Fading Day

Brush strokes paint the sky in hues,
Crimson, gold, and dusky blues.
Clouds drift slowly, dreaming wide,
In the twilight, hopes abide.

Each ray of sun begins to wane,
Nature whispers soft refrain.
Time stands still as colors blend,
Sketches drawn, the day must end.

Shadows stretch on fields of green,
Fingers trace where light has been.
A canvas of moments slips away,
Sketches of a fading day.

In the silence, beauty grows,
As the heart, with twilight, flows.
With each breath, we bid goodbye,
To the wonders of the sky.

Wonder on the Edge of Dusk

At the brink where light must yield,
Secrets of the night revealed.
Curiosity ignites the air,
In the stillness, wonders flare.

Mountains shadowed, whispers low,
A gentle breeze begins to blow.
Every star a story told,
In the twilight, hearts unfold.

Time suspended, softly sways,
Chasing dreams in twilight's haze.
In the quiet, magic hums,
On the edge, the evening comes.

With each heartbeat, we embrace,
Mysteries of the night we chase.
In the dusk, we feel alive,
Wondering where our dreams may thrive.

The Lure of Lunar Light

Underneath the silver glow,
Moonlit paths like rivers flow.
Each step whispers soft and clear,
In lunar light, there's naught to fear.

The world transformed, a portrait bright,
Guided by the starry night.
In stillness, mysteries unveil,
The heart's true song begins to sail.

Dreams take flight on shadows cast,
Fleeting moments, fading fast.
Yet in this glow, we find our place,
The lure of night, a warm embrace.

As the moonlight gently sways,
We're caught in its eternal gaze.
With wonder, we walk this night,
In harmony with lunar light.

Twilight's Gentle Hand

The sun dips low, whispers fade,
Soft shadows stretch, a quiet serenade.
Stars awaken, the sky adorned,
Night's embrace, a longing born.

Colors blend, a dance so rare,
Dreams take flight in evening air.
Moonlight weaves through branches lean,
A tapestry of glimmering sheen.

Crickets sing, the world holds breath,
In twilight's hush, life finds its depth.
Hearts beat softly, futures new,
In this moment, all feels true.

So let us linger in this glow,
As day and night begin to flow.
In twilight's gentle hand we find,
The peace that lingers in our mind.

Mists of the Unseen Hour

Veils of fog on silent streets,
Secrets whisper where daylight meets.
Shadows merge, the world retreats,
In mists of time, the heart repeats.

Footsteps soft on cobblestones,
Echoes linger, haunt the bones.
Veiled figures glide, unseen sway,
In twilight's breath, they drift away.

The air is thick with tales untold,
Of loves lost and dreams of old.
In this realm where visions coalesce,
Mists unveil the heart's deep press.

Through every haze, a truth cuts clear,
In unseen hours, we face our fear.
A shroud of mystery, all around,
In these mists, lost hopes can be found.

Between Day and Night

In that hour where colors blend,
The day recedes, the night will mend.
A gentle sigh, the world stands still,
In twilight's grasp, we feel the thrill.

Fading light on the horizon's crest,
A calm descends, time takes a rest.
Stars emerge like distant dreams,
Illuminated by silver beams.

Between the realms, a fragile line,
Where shadows dance and hearts entwine.
This serenade of dusk and dawn,
In every heartbeat, life is drawn.

So let us wander, hand in hand,
In the twilight's glow, we make our stand.
Between day and night, let us remain,
In whispers soft, we find our gain.

Silhouettes in Silken Hues

Shadows drape on the velvet sky,
Figures dance as time slips by.
Softly shaped by a golden light,
Silhouettes twirl in the coming night.

A hush surrounds, the world feels new,
In colors rich, a lover's view.
Whispers linger, breaths entwined,
In silken hues, our souls aligned.

The gentle breeze, a tender caress,
Guides us closer, hearts confess.
Every moment a soft embrace,
In silhouettes, we find our place.

As darkness falls, dreams take flight,
In the curves of the fading light.
Together we'll share this vibrant glow,
In silken hues, let our love flow.

Murmurs in the Half-Light

Whispers roam through the quiet night,
Shadows dance in soft, gentle flight.
Secrets held in twilight's embrace,
Echoes linger, a soothing trace.

Stars peek through the velvet sky,
Dreams unfurl as moments fly.
In this glow, time gently stirs,
Voices blend with the songs of furs.

Silhouettes of forgotten lore,
Wrap the world with tales of yore.
In half-light, hope softly shines,
Murmurs linger, love aligns.

Here we wander, hearts in tune,
Lost in magic of the moon.
In the hush, our spirits rise,
Murmurs weaving through the sighs.

Pathways of Subtle Radiance

Through the mist, the path unfolds,
Stories of light and shadow told.
Glimmers dance on dew-kissed grass,
Each step taken, moments pass.

Cascades of glimmering dreams,
Illuminating fleeting beams.
In the dark, the luminescence glows,
Whispering secrets only it knows.

Branches arch like welcoming arms,
Nature's grace with all its charms.
In the stillness, soft silence reigns,
Pathways guiding through life's lanes.

Every breath a spark of grace,
Shimmering trails we can trace.
We journey on through gentle light,
In this dance of day and night.

Between Daylight and Stardust

The horizon blushes, day slips away,
Colors mingle in silver and gray.
Between the moments of light and dusk,
Awakens a dream, gentle and husk.

Stars emerge from the blanket of night,
Each a wish, a flickering light.
Softly they speak of worlds afar,
Guiding the hearts like a northern star.

In this space, the whispers grow,
Eternity dances, a rhythmic flow.
Between what was and what shall be,
Time holds its breath, a mystery.

We linger here, souls entwined,
In the canvas, colors aligned.
Amidst the twilight, dreams unfold,
A tapestry woven, stories told.

Reflections of a Dimming Sun

The sun dips low, kissing the sea,
Colors blaze with a tender plea.
Reflections shimmer on waves anew,
As daylight bids its soft adieu.

Crimson skies hold whispers wise,
Secrets linger in evening's sighs.
Each moment graced with golden hues,
A farewell wrapped in softest blues.

In this twilight, shadows play,
A quieter dance at the end of day.
Embers fading, yet spirits soar,
In the twilight glow, we seek for more.

As stars prepare their silver show,
We find warmth in the afterglow.
Let our hearts embrace the night,
In reflections of fading light.

Flickers in the Twilight

Whispers dance upon the breeze,
As daylight fades into the trees.
Shadows stretch and softly sigh,
Beneath the canvas of the sky.

Stars begin their gentle glow,
As twilight paints a world below.
Colors merge in muted hue,
Promises of dreams anew.

In the stillness, hearts will pause,
Lost in wonder, without cause.
Flickers of a fleeting light,
Guide us through the coming night.

Underneath the velvet dome,
Every moment feels like home.
Embracing peace that dusk will bring,
In twilight's arms, the shadows sing.

Between the Here and the Not Yet

Caught in shadows of the past,
Moments linger, never fast.
Footprints left on shifting sand,
Dreams we hold in trembling hand.

Time suspends its gentle flow,
Between the ebb and restless glow.
Paths not taken, dreams deferred,
Silent echoes, softly heard.

A dance of hopes, both near and far,
Guided by a distant star.
Heartbeats quicken with each breath,
Living life between the depths.

In this space, where futures tread,
Every word that's left unsaid.
Build the bridges, weave the thread,
Between the here and what's ahead.

A Murmuration of Shadows

In twilight's hush, the flock appears,
A dance of shadows, drawing near.
Swaying whispers in the air,
Like soft secrets, they declare.

Wings ebb and flow, a portrait drawn,
Forming patterns with the dawn.
Chasing light, they twist and weave,
In this moment, we believe.

Every turn a story told,
In the dark, their shapes unfold.
United voices in the night,
A murmuration, pure delight.

For in the chaos, there's a grace,
A symphony in endless space.
Together, shadows take their flight,
In harmony, through fading light.

Serene Passage to Night's Embrace

As daylight wanes, the stars awaken,
Nature's breath, a law unshaken.
Moonlight spills on quiet streams,
Guiding us to tender dreams.

Breezes sing of calm and peace,
In the darkness, sorrows cease.
A world enveloped in soft sighs,
Where silence whispers lullabies.

Through the pines, a tale unfolds,
Of ancient night, and stories old.
Each step forward, a gentle trace,
On this serene passage to night's embrace.

With every star that lights the way,
Hope ignites the closing day.
In the stillness, hearts align,
As night descends, the soul will shine.

A Tapestry of Silhouettes

In twilight's grip, shadows dance,
Threads of memory, a fleeting chance.
Whispers of dreams on the breeze,
Colors blend beneath the trees.

Moments woven, stitched with care,
Each silhouette, a story to share.
Echoes linger, softly they call,
In this tapestry, we find them all.

Through the night, patterns unfold,
Secrets hidden, tales retold.
A dance of light in the heart's embrace,
A portrait of time, a sacred space.

Time's gentle hand will not unwind,
Yet in these threads, our souls align.
As dawn breaks and shadows flee,
A new day dawns, a chance to be.

Ghosts in the Glow

Under the moon, faces appear,
Whispers echo, drawing near.
Ghostly figures in silver light,
Floating dreams through the night.

Flickering flames, secrets reveal,
Stories hidden, time to heal.
In the glow, they find their voice,
Through the shadows, they've made their choice.

Leaping shadows, dancing free,
In the stillness, hear their plea.
Lost in the night, shadows entwined,
Searching for peace, love undefined.

As dawn breaks, they softly fade,
Leaving echoes of memories made.
In the glow, they live once more,
Ghosts of the past, forever soar.

Gazing into the Fading Abyss

Staring deep into the void,
Where silence reigns and light is coy.
Fleeting visions, shadows cast,
Whispers of futures from the past.

In the stillness, secrets lie,
Waiting for dreams to learn to fly.
Hands reach out, a soft caress,
Amidst the dark, we seek to press.

The abyss beckons, a siren's call,
Drawn to the depths, will we fall?
Eclipsed by doubt, hope lingers near,
In this darkness, we face our fear.

Glimmers of light begin to gleam,
Awakening the heart's wild dream.
Together we'll rise, defy the night,
In the fading abyss, we'll find our light.

The Ascent of the Evening Star

As twilight whispers, colors blend,
A journey starts, on paths we wend.
The evening star, a beacon bright,
Guiding us through the coming night.

With every step, the world aglow,
A shimmering trail where dreams can flow.
Silent wishes on a breeze,
Carried forth with grace and ease.

Honoring the night as shadows fall,
The star ascends, it beckons all.
With open hearts, we chase the glow,
In this magic, we come to know.

The cosmos hums a soothing tune,
Under the watch of a silver moon.
Together we rise, hand in hand,
The evening star, our promised land.

The Fading Day's Embrace

The sun dips low with golden light,
A whisper soft, day turns to night.
Colors swirl in the twilight glow,
As shadows lengthen, dreams begin to flow.

The breeze carries tales of day,
Hints of laughter now drift away.
Stars peek out, shy and bright,
In the calming hush of approaching night.

Crickets sing their evening song,
Nature's chorus, where we belong.
A fleeting moment, time stands still,
Wrapped in dusk's gentle, tender thrill.

In fading rays, a night's embrace,
We find solace in a secret space.
The day may fade, but hearts will stay,
In the warmth of this fading day.

Secrets of the Dim Horizon

Beyond the dusk, where shadows play,
The horizon holds secrets of the day.
Veils of mist drape the quiet land,
Whispers linger, soft and unplanned.

The world grows dim, yet eyes remain,
Searching for beauty in the mundane.
Each stitch of twilight, a palette divine,
Drawing us closer, the stars align.

Hidden wonders come into view,
In the soft glow of the fading blue.
Each breath a promise, the night unfurls,
Dreams take flight, as mystery swirls.

Linger here on this edge of sight,
Where day meets night, and wrong meets right.
In silence, the universe starts to sing,
A symphony of secrets, the night will bring.

Starlit Wanderings

Under a canopy of velvet skies,
We wander 'neath the stars that rise.
Each twinkle tells a story old,
Of dreams pursued and hearts that bold.

Footsteps echo on the cool night air,
Mysterious paths lead everywhere.
A journey whispered on the breeze,
Inviting souls to seek and tease.

With every star, a wish is cast,
In the starlit glow, the shadows are vast.
Lost in wonder, where we belong,
In the serenade of night's sweet song.

The universe speaks in quiet tones,
In starlit wanderings, we find our homes.
Together we map the celestial maze,
In the shimmering dance of the night's soft haze.

Evening's Soft Serenade

As the sun slips beneath the seas,
The evening hums with gentle breeze.
A melody swells in the twilight air,
Carrying whispers of love and care.

The sky blushes in shades of rose,
An artist's brush where silence flows.
Every note in the night softly strays,
In evening's arms, we lose our ways.

Stars twinkle like notes on a page,
Each one a tale from a distant age.
In this serenade, hearts are laid bare,
Wrapped in the warmth that night can wear.

Let us dance under the fading light,
As evening's song drapes us tight.
In whispers sweet, our dreams collide,
In this soft serenade, we shall abide.

The Silent Passage of Evening

The sun dips low, a fleeting glow,
Whispers of night begin to flow.
Soft shadows stretch, embrace the day,
In hushed tones, the light slips away.

Crickets chirp their evening song,
As dusk unfurls, it won't be long.
Stars awaken in the deepening blue,
The night reveals a dream come true.

Moonlight bathes the world below,
Guiding hearts through the ebb and flow.
In the quiet, secrets blend,
A serenade that never ends.

With each breath, the moments cease,
In the evening's warm release.
We find solace in night's embrace,
In the stillness, we find our place.

Reflections in the Softening Glow

Golden hues upon the lake,
Rippling gently, dreams awake.
The sun surrenders, shadows grow,
In the warmth of the softening glow.

Gentle winds through willow trees,
Whisper secrets, carry ease.
Fading light meets the water's grace,
Mirrored memories, a sacred space.

Clouds drift softly, painted skies,
Where colors dance, and hope will rise.
In this embrace, all burdens shed,
Reflections lead where hearts are led.

Time stands still in twilight's clasp,
A fleeting moment meant to last.
Through fading light, our spirits soar,
In the glow, we seek for more.

Twilight's Whispering Dreams

As daylight fades, the stars align,
In twilight's grasp, our dreams entwine.
Softly painted with shades of night,
A canvas rich, where visions light.

Cicadas sing their lullabies,
Underneath the velvet skies.
In the twilight's gentle hold,
Whispered promises unfold.

Figures dance in shadows cast,
Moments linger, shadows past.
With every sigh, the night awakes,
In dreams where the heart gently breaks.

Time bows low in this serene hour,
Nature's grace, a timeless power.
In twilight's glow, we come alive,
Where whispered dreams so sweetly thrive.

Beneath the Lavender Sky

Lavender clouds in evening's embrace,
Drifting slowly, a tranquil space.
As colors blend in a soft array,
Peaceful moments softly sway.

The horizon blushes in silken hue,
A promise made, each day anew.
With every breath beneath this dome,
We wander far, we find our home.

Stars sprinkle hope like fairy dust,
In the quiet, we learn to trust.
Underneath the vast expanse,
We dance through time, a fleeting chance.

In lavender light, dreams interlace,
As night descends with gentle grace.
We gather moments, heartbeats fly,
Forever bound beneath the lavender sky.

A Glimpse of Glistening Shadows

In twilight's hush, shadows creep,
Glistening soft, secrets they keep.
Whispers of night, they start to sway,
Painting the world in muted gray.

Behind the trees, they play and hide,
Secrets shared on the moonlit tide.
With gentle grace, they spin and twirl,
A dance of darkness, a silent whirl.

Beneath the stars, a story unfolds,
Of dreams and fears, of hopes untold.
Glimmers of light, a silver thread,
In the heart of night, where all is said.

As shadows fade with the coming dawn,
Their sparkle lingers, yet they are gone.
A glimpse of magic, fleeting and bright,
In the arms of the welcoming night.

Stars Unfurling at Dusk

As day whispers close, the sky ignites,
Stars unfurling in velvet nights.
They shimmer softly, a cosmic song,
Guiding the dreamers as they belong.

In the hush of dusk, they start to gleam,
Each tiny beacon, a vibrant dream.
Like scattered petals on midnight's breeze,
They dance and twirl with elegant ease.

Moonlight brushes the earth so light,
A canvas where shadows take flight.
With every twinkle, stories are spun,
Echoes of night, where the day is done.

In this quiet space, hearts find their way,
In the embrace of night, they choose to stay.
Whispers of starlight, secrets to own,
In the vast expanse, we are never alone.

The Last Breath of Color

As the sun dips low, the colors blend,
A palette of dreams at the day's end.
Crimson and gold, a fleeting embrace,
In the fading light, we find our place.

The last breath of color, a soft sigh,
Kissing the horizon, bidding goodbye.
Clouds wrapped in hues like stories told,
With memories woven in threads of gold.

In twilight's grip, shadows grow long,
Nature's symphony, a fading song.
Each hue a promise, each shade a prayer,
In the canvas of dusk, beauty laid bare.

As day turns to night, the colors wane,
But in our hearts, their legacy remains.
The last breath of color, a gentle goodnight,
In the embrace of the soft twilight.

Shadows Dancing with Nightfall

When night descends, the shadows sway,
Dancing softly, leading the way.
They blend with the stars, a delicate blend,
In the silence, they twist and bend.

Under the cloak of the moon's soft light,
Shadows gather, shimmering bright.
In playful arcs, they spin around,
Whispers of secrets in silence found.

Each flicker a tale of moments past,
Of laughter, of love, memories cast.
With every movement, they come alive,
As night unfolds, the dark will thrive.

As dawn approaches, they start to fade,
Yet in the heart, their dance is laid.
Shadows of night, forever they'll stay,
In the echoes of light, they'll gently play.

In the Half-Light's Embrace

Shadows twine like whispers soft,
As daylight fades, hearts lift aloft.
Dreams awaken in twilight's sway,
In the half-light's embrace, we stay.

Stars blink slowly, a tender glow,
Echoes of dusk in the night's flow.
Paths less traveled, mysteries bloom,
In this gentle twilight, there's room.

Moonlight drapes the world in grace,
Every sigh finds its sacred place.
Feeling the pulse of silence near,
In the half-light, nothing to fear.

Time stands still, as night takes hold,
Whispers of secrets, quietly told.
In the embrace where shadows blend,
A soft farewell, as day does end.

Steps on the Dim Trail

Bare feet tread on a winding path,
Beneath the trees, the shadows bath.
Moonlight dances through branches tall,
Sharing secrets in the night's enthrall.

Echoes linger of forgotten dreams,
Where soft winds play and the starlight beams.
Each step whispers of stories past,
On the dim trail, memories cast.

Crickets serenade, a lullaby soft,
The world slows down, the spirits loft.
With every heartbeat, the night unfolds,
Steps on the dim trail, timeless and bold.

Faint echoes of laughter, lost to the air,
Though the journey is lonely, none seem to care.
In the magic of night, every traveler sways,
On dim trails of wonder, we wander our ways.

Secrets of the Dimming Day

As the sun dips low, colors fade,
Softly whispers an evening serenade.
Clouds blush gently in hues of gray,
Holding close the secrets of the day.

Rays retreat with a peaceful sigh,
Casting long shadows as time slips by.
Every moment, a treasure stored,
In the twilight, our hearts are floored.

Night unveils what daylight kept,
In twilight's gaze, the world has slept.
Each star a story, each breeze a song,
Secrets of the dimming day belong.

Silence deepens as shadows conspire,
In this gentle dusk, we find our fire.
Embrace the night, let your worries stray,
In twilight's embrace, secrets won't sway.

A Dance with the Dusk

Twilight whispers, its softest call,
Calling forth shadows to dance and enthrall.
As the sun bows low, a painter's brush,
Colors swirl in a magical hush.

Beneath the sky's changing tapestry,
We move like leaves in a waltz set free.
With every heartbeat, the world spins slow,
In the dusk's embrace, we let feelings flow.

Nature hums a lullaby sweet,
In the fading light, our hearts do meet.
With a gentle sway, we drift and glide,
In this dance with dusk, we confide.

As stars emerge, the night takes flight,
Holding our stories in the dark's light.
With each step whispered, dreams intertwine,
A dance with the dusk, where souls align.

A Lament for Lost Light

The sun descends with heavy sighs,
Shadows stretch where laughter lies.
Once bright days now fade to gray,
Echoes linger of a brighter day.

Memories dance like flickered flame,
Whispers softly call my name.
In twilight's grasp, I stand alone,
A heart grown weary, a chilling tone.

The stars emerge, one by one,
Promising hope with the rising moon.
Yet each glow feels like a ghost,
A fading warmth, a fleeting host.

So here I weep for light once dear,
In the silence, I find my fear.
For every day must meet this night,
And mourn the loss of cherished light.

Echoing Silence of Dusk

The sky turns soft, a muted hue,
Daylight bows, the night feels new.
Gentle breezes brush my cheek,
In the stillness, shadows speak.

Fading whispers, secrets shared,
Memories weave of love declared.
In the hush where time stands still,
Hope lingers on, a subtle thrill.

Stars awaken, twinkling bright,
Guardians of the velvet night.
They watch over with tender grace,
Cradling dreams in their embrace.

The world feels calm, yet somehow vast,
In twilight's glow, the moments pass.
With every breath, I find my place,
In the echoing silence, a warm embrace.

Colors of the Evening Tide

Crimson waves crash on the shore,
As daylight yields to night once more.
The sky ignites in vibrant song,
A canvas painted, bold and strong.

Lavender hues begin to blend,
Where day and night in dance transcend.
Footsteps mark the sandy trail,
Stories woven, lost in the gale.

Golden hues turn soft and pale,
Reflections shimmer, then set sail.
Each color speaks of love and loss,
A fleeting moment, an endless toss.

As dusk enfolds the world in grace,
I find my heart in this warm place.
The evening tide, a soft goodbye,
Whispers linger, 'neath the vast sky.

On the Brink of Nightfall

The horizon swells with shades of gray,
As daylight fades, it slips away.
In the twilight, secrets dare,
To breathe beneath the evening air.

Candles flicker in the gloaming,
While the whispering winds keep roaming.
Footsteps echo in the quiet,
Spirits gather, soft and riot.

Through tangled roots of ancient trees,
The world is laced with mysteries.
Nightfall beckons, time to dream,
In the shadows, life may gleam.

The stars above begin to twinkle,
A silent dance, their light will sprinkle.
On the brink of night, we wait,
For the magic that must create.

The Prelude to Stars

In the hush of night, dreams take flight,
Soft whispers linger, hearts ignite.
Silent wishes dance in the air,
Beneath the moon's soft, tender glare.

A canvas painted with shimmering light,
Each star a story, a guiding sight.
Galaxies swirl in a cosmic waltz,
In this moment, we find no faults.

Echoes of laughter, sweet serenades,
Radiate warmth as daylight fades.
The prelude to dreams, so sweetly spun,
Awaits the embrace of night's gentle fun.

In this twilight, wonders unfold,
Adventures await, stories untold.
With each shimmering glow, we embark,
On a journey ignited by spark.

Mysteries of the Gentle Shadows

In the corners where shadows play,
Lies a secret in the fading day.
Tales of whispers, soft and low,
Dancing lightly, like winter snow.

The world transformed in twilight's hue,
Colors mingling, old and new.
Gentle sighs in the hush of night,
Reveal the dreams that take their flight.

Branches sway with a knowing grace,
Hidden stories in their embrace.
Mysteries linger in every nook,
If you listen close, you'll hear them crook.

In the shadows, life softly creeps,
A tapestry woven, where nature sleeps.
Every heartbeat, a fleeting sound,
In the stillness, our hopes are found.

Whispers at Dusk

As daylight fades, the world grows still,
Whispers at dusk, a secret thrill.
Colors blend, a soft reframed glow,
In this moment, time starts to slow.

Crickets sing their twilight song,
A lullaby where dreams belong.
Breezes carry tales from afar,
Each star twinkles, a guiding star.

Fleeting moments, the day's sweet breath,
In quiet corners, life feels fresh.
With heavy hearts, we release our sighs,
Under the embrace of darkening skies.

Dusk wraps its arms, soft and tight,
Inviting us deeper into the night.
Letting go of what may be lost,
In the silence, we take the cost.

Shadows Beneath the Twilight Sky

Beneath the canvas of twilight's hue,
Shadows gather, a cloak of blue.
Secrets whispered in the soft night air,
Hidden laughter, glimpses rare.

As stars awaken, dreams arise,
Stories shimmer in the velvet skies.
Nature breathes in harmony's song,
In the darkness, we all belong.

The twilight dances, a gentle sway,
Merging colors as night takes the day.
In the quiet, we feel the pulse,
Of life and love, an endless impulse.

With shadows around, we walk so near,
Embracing hopes, releasing fear.
Under the twilight, hearts align,
In the hush of night, forever entwined.

Chasing the Last Gleam

The sun dips low in the sky,
Colors bleed as day bids goodbye.
Chasing shadows that dance and weave,
I follow the light that I believe.

Whispers of dusk begin to sigh,
A fleeting moment as it slips by.
With every step, the warmth retreats,
Yet in my heart, the light still beats.

Fingers reach for the fading ray,
In the twilight, dreams come to play.
A path of gold, oh so divine,
Chasing the last gleam, your hand in mine.

As darkness swells, I won't despair,
For in each shadow, love will share.
Together we'll find where stars ignite,
In the embrace of the coming night.

Beneath the Veil of Night

Beneath the veil of night so deep,
Where secrets stir and shadows creep.
The moon, a lantern in the dark,
Guides lost wanderers with its spark.

Trees stand tall, their branches sway,
In whispers soft, the night will play.
A symphony of crickets sings,
While gentle breezes weave through wings.

Each star twinkles a tale untold,
In the quiet, wild dreams unfold.
Beneath the veil, we come alive,
In the hush of night, our spirits thrive.

The world outside softly fades away,
In this cocoon, we'll choose to stay.
With hearts entwined, the darkness glows,
Beneath the night, our love just grows.

A Realm of Soft Shadows

In a realm of soft shadows cast,
Memories linger, echoes of the past.
Whispers of light play hide and seek,
In this twilight, silence speaks.

Dreams drift lightly upon the breeze,
Carried away with graceful ease.
Each moment captured in twilight's embrace,
A dance of time, a sacred space.

The stars emerge to paint the sky,
With shimmering tales as we sigh.
In this realm where shadows meet,
Our hearts unite, a rhythm sweet.

As night unfolds its velvet cloak,
We find the words left unspoken.
With every glance, we weave our fate,
In this world where love won't wait.

Nightfall's Gentle Touch

Nightfall whispers with tender grace,
Wrapping the world in a soft embrace.
The day surrenders, bows its head,
While dreams awaken from their bed.

The sky dons stars like golden lace,
A tranquil touch in this vast space.
Moonlight dances on silent streams,
Illuminating all our dreams.

Silent wishes drift through the air,
In the calm, we breathe without a care.
Nightfall's beauty, a gentle muse,
In its glow, our hearts we choose.

Together we stand, hand in hand,
In this moment, we'll make our stand.
With every heartbeat, love will flow,
As night wraps us in its soft glow.

Milton Keynes UK
Ingram Content Group UK Ltd.
UKHW030750121124
451094UK00013B/797

9 789916 908198